My Mom the Mayor

ANGELA
CABRILLA

FOR
MAYOR

Robert Hillman
Illustrated by Naomi Lewis

Contents

Chapter 1 Mom's Great Idea 4

Chapter 2 Mom's Surprise 10

Chapter 3 Getting Serious 16

Chapter 4 The Debate 22

Chapter 5 My Mom the Mayor 28

The Facts Behind the Story 31

Extend Your Reading 32

Chapter 1

Mom's Great Idea

I live in a place called Los Aguas. It's a very small town, so it might not seem like a big deal that my mom was running for mayor. It's not like running for president, or congress, or governor. But believe me, it really *was* a big deal. For example, there was stuff like Jimmy Berg's new bike. But I'll get back to that.

Los Aguas is down on the river. The town used to be right in the middle of cattle country. There were cotton farms nearby, too. There are still some cattle ranches, but the old cotton mills by the river are gone now. So things have changed a little. But the town does okay.

My mom has a restaurant on Main Street.
I help out there after school and on weekends.

It was spring when Mom had her great idea. We were out riding our bikes, Mom and I. We do that after we close the restaurant in the afternoon. We were riding on a busy road near the river. The river looked great.

I remembered what the river was like after the old cotton mills were torn down. Bricks were scattered all over. Weeds grew on the empty land. It looked bad.

Then people from Los Aguas fixed all that. My mom got the whole thing going. We cleaned up the land. We planted reeds and grass, and water birds came back to nest in the reeds. My mom also wanted the town to build a bicycle path down there for everyone to use.

But let me get back to the story. Like I said, we were riding our bikes. Then we saw a huge, new sign right there on the riverbank.

Coming Soon!
20 Luxury Riverfront Homes!
Call Ron Holiday
Holiday Homes

"Hey!" Mom said. "They can't build houses here! What about the bike path?"

"Right, there won't be room for big houses *and* a bike path," I agreed.

We stood there beside our bikes. I could see Mom was really angry. She was quiet all the way home.

After supper, she said, "Monica,
Election Day is in November. That's when
we vote for mayor, the person who runs the
town government."

"That's right," I said.

"I've got an idea, Monica. A great idea.
I've been thinking about it for months," she
said. She had a strange look in her eyes.

"So, what's your idea, Mom?" I asked.

"I'll surprise you," she said mysteriously.

Chapter 2

Mom's Surprise

Mom did surprise me. When I got to the restaurant after school, she was standing behind the counter. She looked excited. Mrs. Berg from the bookshop next door was there, and she looked excited, too. Her son Jimmy was out on the sidewalk with his new red bike. Jimmy loved his bike but hardly ever got a chance to ride it.

"You should be very proud of your mom, Monica!" said Mrs. Berg.

"Why?" I asked.

"She's running for mayor!" she replied.

"For mayor? But Ron Holiday's the mayor! You can't beat Happy Holiday!" I exclaimed. This was a big surprise!

"Now, Monica," said Mom, as she smiled, "as a citizen, it's my right to run for mayor. The mayor is supposed to take care of this town, and Mr. Holiday isn't doing his job."

"We need that bike path," said Mrs. Berg. "Where else can Jimmy ride his bike safely? We bought him the bike when Mayor Holiday had plans to build a bike path on the land along the river. But now that plan has changed! Happy is more interested in selling the land to the company that wants to build big houses on the river."

Let me explain something. Happy Holiday's real name is Ron Holiday, but everyone calls him Happy. He owns Holiday Homes on Main Street and his slogan is, *Move right into a Holiday Home!* Some people don't think he's such a great mayor, but they vote for him anyway because he's so friendly. Besides, nobody else has run for mayor in years.

When Mom and I went for a bike ride
that evening, I saw more and more things
that needed to be fixed. Fairview Park was
run-down. The playground equipment
needed to be replaced. The skateboard
ramp hadn't been finished.

When I thought about it later, I could see that my mom would be a very good mayor. She was always thinking about the town and making things happen, like fixing the riverbank and planning a bike path. She talked to all the people who came into the restaurant. She knew what people really wanted for the town.

Chapter 3

Getting Serious

Back home, Mom read the list of all the things the mayor does.

Leads city council meetings

Attends important town events

Creates committees and appoints members

Makes yearly report on the town

Signs all new laws

Approves the town budget

The list went on and on. We soon realized that being mayor is more than just getting a bike path in town!

"You're going to be very busy if you're mayor, Mom," I said.

"We can afford to hire part-time help for the restaurant," Mom said. "But I'll need your help if I'm going to win, Monica."

"Okay, Mom," I said. "I'll help."

We had a lot to do before the election. I got all my friends to help. My mom printed a lot of flyers and posters, and we passed them out. There was information about how a bike path would be good for the town, and a picture of my mom looking serious.

Mom and I knocked on doors and talked to neighbors about the town. But people weren't all that interested.

"Do you really think things are that bad, Angela?" they asked.

We set up a great website with pictures of places in the town that needed improvement.

Not many people visited the website. Mom just couldn't get her message across. People started calling her *Angry Angela*.

When Mom was interviewed on our local TV station she talked about all the things she could do for the town. I thought she did really well.

Then Happy came on.

"Angela, you sound like you want to live someplace else," he said. "Me, I love this town. I love the people here. I wouldn't live anywhere else in the whole world."

That wasn't good! Happy was going to
get votes because he was so nice to
everyone, not because he had plans to
make our town better! I thought we had
lost our chance to win the election.

Chapter 4

The Debate

Then one day, Mr. Berg stopped by the restaurant. Like Mom, he thought there were some things in the town that needed to be fixed.

"You know what could help, Angela?" Mr. Berg said. "A debate. In a debate, you and Happy can discuss your ideas. The citizens of Los Aguas can listen and decide whose ideas they like better. I'm sure they'll like yours."

Happy agreed to have a debate. I guess he was pretty sure he could beat Mom. Mr. Berg helped organize it. The date was set for three weeks before Election Day.

Mom got ready for the debate. She surveyed people to find out what else they were worried about. Now she didn't look angry. She just looked like she cared about the town.

On the night of the debate, a big crowd turned out. Mom and Happy sat up on stage with a big flag on each side.

Before the debate started, I whispered to Mom, "Good luck!"

"Monica, I'm nervous!" she said.

"You'll be great, Mom!" I replied.

Naturally, I was on her side. After all, she's my mom, and I love her. But anyone will tell you, Angela Cabrilla was great. She did a special presentation showing everyone how much money the city collects through taxes. She also showed where that money goes, and how some of it is wasted. She showed people how she would use the money in a better way.

She spoke about committees that the mayor is in charge of, like the park committee and the library committee. She had a plan for everything, including the bike path.

"In my plan," Mom said, "the company can build smaller houses, further back from the river, and leave plenty of space for a bike path. That way, everyone is a winner, not just people buying and selling houses."

She also told the story of how little Jimmy Berg had a new red bike but nowhere to ride it because the town didn't have a bike path.

Somebody asked Happy about the potholes in the streets, the skateboard ramp, and the run-down playground at Fairview Park.

"Well, I was going to get around to fixing all of that," Happy said, but for once, he didn't look so happy.

Chapter 5

My Mom the Mayor

After that debate, lots of people wanted to help Mom—even kids! They loved the bike path plan. Some people made new posters, with a much better picture. They told their neighbors to vote for Mom. Suddenly, Mom's campaign was the happiest thing in the whole town.

Mom won by 800 votes on Election Day. I went with her to her first meeting with the city council. Now, six months have passed since the election. The skateboard ramp is ready. Every streetlight in Los Aguas works. And the potholes are gone.

The bike path was finished and opened just last Saturday—thanks to my mom the mayor. And do you know who was first to use it? Jimmy Berg. Mom made sure of that!

Voting in Elections

Citizens vote to elect government leaders. In the United States, citizens who are 18 years and older have the right to vote. They vote on Election Day. The votes are counted to find out who has won the election.

Before Election Day, there is a campaign. People who want to be government leaders talk about their ideas. A campaign can help citizens decide who to vote for.

These citizens are going to vote for their government leaders.

Think About the Story

In *My Mom the Mayor*, Monica's mom, Angela, runs for mayor and wins the election. Think about these questions.

- Why does Monica's mom decide to run for mayor? What does she want to do for her community?
- How do Monica and her mom tell people about new ideas for the town?
- What happens when Angela and Happy Holiday have a debate? Why is the debate important?

To read more about communities and government, read the books below.

SUGGESTED READING
Windows on Literacy
Serving the Community
Symbols of Freedom